c.2

E
Man   Manley, Deborah
           Around the house

Around the House

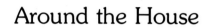

Library of Congress Number: 78-31854

 3 4 5 6 7 8 9 0

Printed in the United States of America.

Library of Congress Cataloging in Publication Data

Manley, Deborah.
  Around the house.

  SUMMARY: Encourages the reader to examine,
think about, and describe objects and places in and
around the house.
  1. Dwellings — Juvenile literature. 2. Home —
Juvenile literature. [1. Dwellings] I. Maclean,
Moira. II. Maclean, Colin. III. Title.
TH4811.5.M36 640 78-31854
ISBN 0-8172-1307-4 lib. bdg.

Around the House

Words by
Deborah Manley

Pictures by
Moira and Colin Maclean

RAINTREE CHILDRENS BOOKS
Milwaukee · Toronto · Melbourne · London

Here is a house. This is the front
of the house. What colors do you
see?

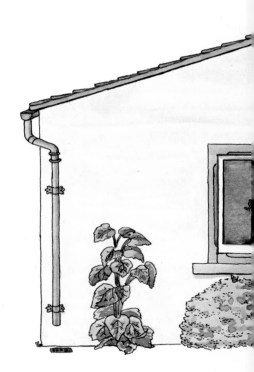

6

Here is the back of the house.
Can you see the family that lives
here? How many are in the
family? How many children?

What is the girl taking out of the
pond? What is the other girl using
to gather the leaves? What is the
boy doing? What is the dog
chasing?

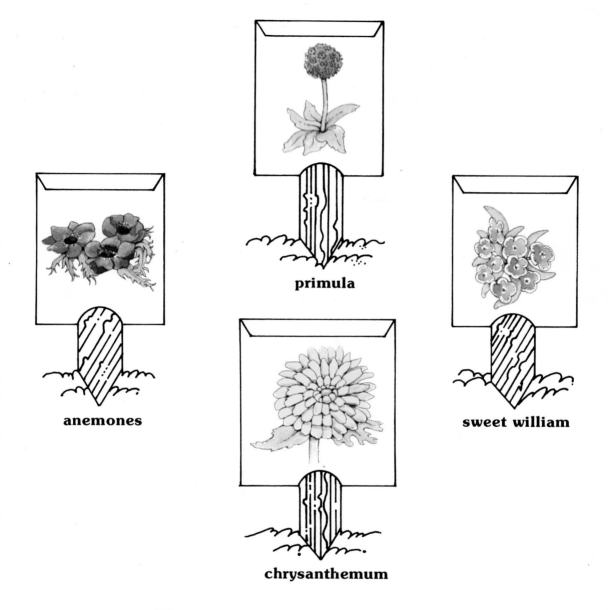

primula

anemones

sweet william

chrysanthemum

Here are some flowers that grow
in the garden. What are their names?

Look at the rows of vegetables
growing in the garden. How many
rows are there? What kind of
vegetable has the boy pulled out
of the ground?

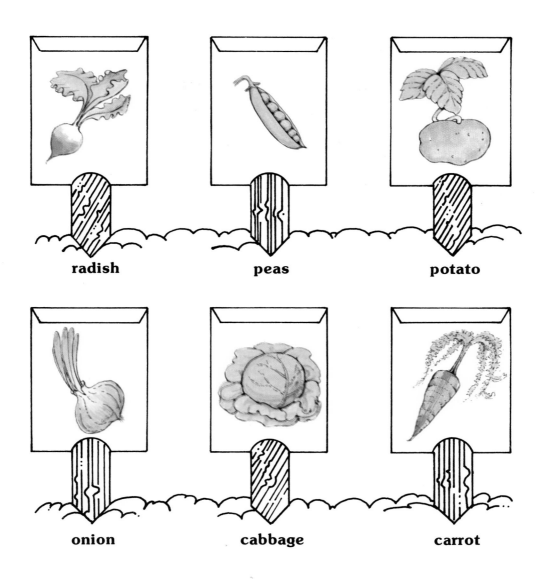

radish peas potato

onion cabbage carrot

Name some vegetables that grow under the ground. Which ones grow on top? Which vegetables do you like to eat?

Let's look at the inside of the house. How many rooms are there? What are the rooms called?

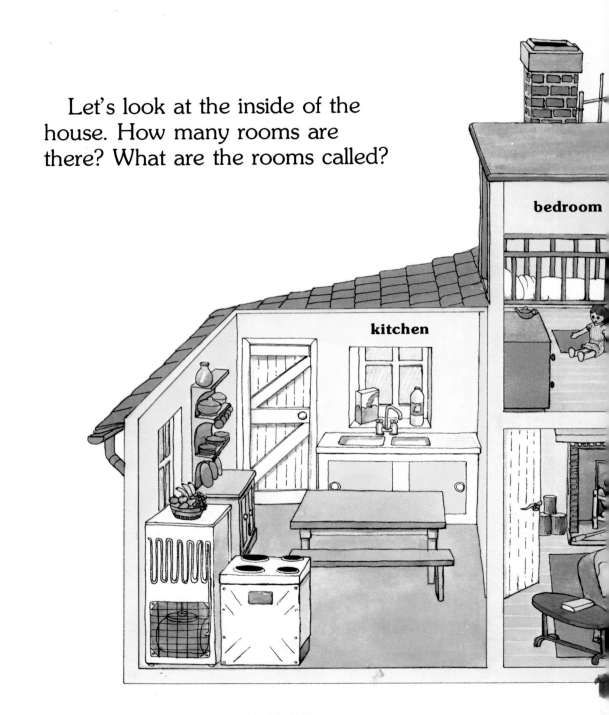

bedroom

kitchen

12

bathroom

living room

hall

13

Look at the pictures on this page. Which rooms would you find these things in? How many things are there?

Tell what each thing is. What color is the cup? Which thing tells time? Which thing could you sit on?

The family is inside the house.
What rooms are they in? What is
each person doing? In which room
is the dog being fed? Are there any
rooms that are empty?

The children are in the living room.
Tell what each child is doing.

Each child is playing with a toy.
Follow the colored lines with your
finger to find which toy each child
is playing with.

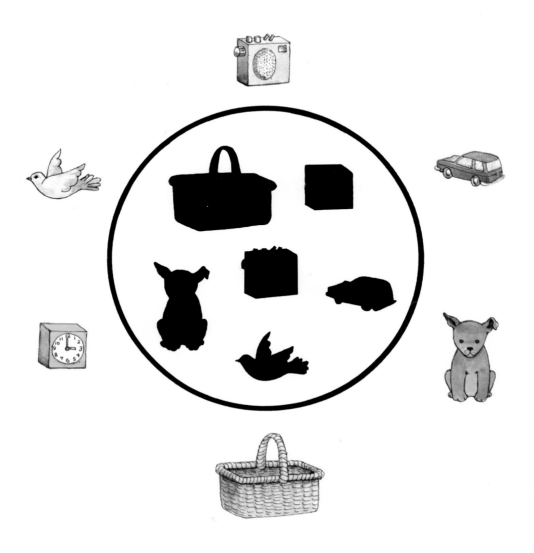

Look at the pictures on the outside of the circle. Now find the black shape inside the circle that is the same as each picture.

The family is in the kitchen.
They are making a pie. How many
people are there? How many
animals?

Which room do you see in this picture? Is the room upstairs or downstairs?

Can you find these things in the picture of the room? How many things are there? What color is the plate?

Look at the picture of this room.
See if you can find the toy duck.
Can you find the other things?
What can you find that is blue?

The children are tired after a long day. Father is going to read a story to them.

Do you have a favorite story?

This will help you with the Word Review.

a	**a** as in **cat**
ā	**a** as in **able**
ä	**a** as in **father**
e	**e** as in **bend**
ē	**e** as in **me**
i	**i** as in **in**
ī	**i** as in **ice**
o	**o** as in **top**
ō	**o** as in **old**
ô	**o** as in **cloth**
oo	**oo** as in **good**
oo	**oo** as in **tool**
oi	**oi** as in **oil**
ou	**ou** as in **out**
u	**u** as in **up**
ur	**ur** as in **fur**
yoo	**u** as in **use**
ə	**a** as in **again**
ch	**ch** as in **such**
ng	**ng** as in **sing**
sh	**sh** as in **shell**
th	**th** as in **three**
th	**th** as in **that**

Word Review

Here are some words from *Around the House*. Practice saying each word out loud. See if you can find them in the book.

anemone (ə nem′ ə nē)
bathroom (bath′ r͞oom′)
bedroom (bed′ r͞oom′)
cabbage (kab′ ij)
chrysanthemum (krə san′ thə məm)
downstairs (doun′ sterz′)
hall (hôl)
living room (liv′ ing r͞oom)
onion (un′ yən)
pea (pē)
primula (prim′ yə lə)
radish (rad′ ish)
sweet william (swēt wil′ yəm)
upstairs (up′ sterz′)